This book belongs to

____

Maxy-Moo Flies to the Moon

Published by BoomerMax Ltd

Prepress by Lighthouse24

ISBN: 978-0-473-38880-5 (paperback)
ISBN: 978-0-473-38882-9 (hardcover)
ISBN: 978-0-473-38883-6 (Kindle)

A catalogue record for this book is available from the National Library of New Zealand.

For Max - your imagination knows no bounds - Julie

For Moana - Catty

Maxy-Moo Flies to the Moon

Story by Julie Schooler
Pictures by Catty Flores

"Maxy-Moo, it's time for bed!"

"No!" he stomps, shaking his head.

"No bed yet, it's way too soon.

Instead, I want to fly to the moon."

Tape and crayons from his pocket
help a box become a rocket.
Blast off! Maxy's rocket flies,
zooming through the starry skies.

Landing on the moon is bumpy.
Lots of rocks, they're big and lumpy.
"Welcome Maxy" says the Moon.
"Join the party, starting soon."

Maxy sees a friendly face.
His favorite playmate, here in space.
Flynn says "Hey there Maxy-Moo,
follow me, I've found a zoo!"

The boys run over to discover –

it's a zoo, but like no other.

Animals all get along...

There's even
dancing
AND
music
AND...

...a big sing-along!

It's all the babies that won't sleep.
Chickens, horses, cows and sheep.
On a speedy spaceship flight
to the moon for disco night!

From elephants to tiny frogs,
cats and mice and barking dogs.
Tigers, lions, cockatoos,
lizards, ducks and kangaroos.

They are babies but look scary.
Max and Flynn are feeling wary.
“They’re just young,” the Moon says quickly.
“Not yet fierce, rough or prickly.”

Flynn and Maxy take a chance -
they say hello and join the dance.
They sing with meerkats, hop with hares,
swing with monkeys, skip with bears.

A conga line, led by a yak
attracts the boys, they join the back.
Jokes are told, the creatures laugh.
The fun delights a shy giraffe.

But soon the youngsters rub their eyes.

Now they're saying their good-byes.

With eyelids drooping down like lead,
the boys fly home and straight to bed.

The moon is shining soft and bright.

Sleepy Maxy says "Good night."

About the Author

Julie Schooler is an author, blogger, speaker and mama of two beautiful tiny humans. Her non-fiction books provide straightforward information on parenting topics. This is her first picture book.

Connect with her at CherishMama.com

Easy Peasy Potty Training

Easy Peasy Healthy Eating

About the Illustrator

Catty Flores is a Spanish illustrator, character designer and storyboard artist. After living in London for the past decade she is now enjoying and exploring the southern hemisphere. Catty's artistic playmates have included international publishing houses and advertising agencies.

Check out her latest creations at CattyFlores.com

PLEASE LEAVE A REVIEW

Thanks for choosing this book to read to your tiny human.

One more favor – please leave a helpful and honest review (a sentence or two is enough) so that it can help other busy parents choose this book as their go-to bedtime story.

Click into Amazon, Goodreads or wherever you purchased this book from to leave a review today.

Made in the USA
Coppell, TX
23 September 2021

62824648R00021